LETTERS TO MY
DAUGHTER

A Mother's Parenting Journey
Through the Classic Exchange
of Letter Writing

RAQUEL MILTON

LETTERS TO MY
DAUGHTER

A Mother's Parenting Journey Through the Classic Exchange of
Letter Writing

RAQUEL MILTON

CITI OF
BOOKS

CITIOFBOOKS, INC.
3736 Eubank NE Suite A1
Albuquerque, NM 87111-3579
www.citiofbooks.com
Hotline: 1 (877) 389-2759
Fax: 1 (505) 930-7244

Ordering Information:

Quantity sales. Special discounts are available on quantity purchases by corporations, associations, and others. For details, contact the publisher at the address above.

Printed in the United States of America.

ISBN-13: Paperback   979-8-89391-563-1
          eBook   979-8-89391-564-8

Library of Congress Control Number: 2025903881

Table of Contents

I dedicate this book to my daughter, Maria, who has been a wonderful gift to me, as a mother. Thank you for your respect, love, and understanding as we matured together through the years as mother and daughter. Your tenacity, resilience and genuine love for people has always been an inspiration to me in my own life's journey. I hope that my written words and prayers through the years have sustained you in fulfilling God's purpose for your life. Love, Peace and Prosperity,

Your Mom,

Introduction

I was inspired to write this book in memory of my mother, Daisy Ballard Cobbins, who devoted her life to her family, her church and her community; but especially to her children. I am grateful to my Mom for putting before me such a perfect example of motherhood and womanhood and showed me the true meaning of spirituality.

This book emerges from a deep desire to share my experience of raising my daughter. I can honestly say that my parenting journey has been bitter-sweet but extremely rewarding. Let me go on record to say that there is no official handbook for parenting. The discipline of Parenting should fit in the category of on-the-job training. When a child is born, so is a parent. They simultaneously grow together.

The role of parenting is a calling. Just as ministers are called to preach and lead a flock or congregation, parents are called to provide and guide. A calling may not necessarily be easy or what you would have chosen for yourself at that appointed time; but it is something that you would never want to end, abandon or taken away from you.

There is no absolute formula for raising a child. But I truly believe that certain tools can be used to make the journey less rocky. The tool that I chose time after time to communicate with my daughter was letter-writing. This tactic became natural to me, considering that my own mother, Daisy Ballard Cobbins, was, too, a devout letter-writer. Over the years, this communication technique of writing transitioned from handwritten letters, to type-written letters, to computer generated letters, to e-mails and text messages. The impact of communicating your deepest thoughts without interruption or uncontrolled emotion while having a captive audience is invaluable. My journey begins with one of my favorite letters that my mother wrote to me a month before my 18th birthday on June 20, 1983.

My Dear Raquel,

I'm in my room, here at Notre Dame University, looking out of my window and thinking about my beautiful family at home. I really miss you. I particularly thought of you when I saw or noticed the giant statue of the Virgin Mary in the distance. She or it stands gallantly against the crystal-clear sky with birds delighting themselves at her feet. She shares everything and enjoys peace. The stillness and intellectual atmosphere is to be admired. Of course, all of the students are home now, and we have full run of the campus here.

You have made me proud of you, all of your life. I have never been disappointed in your decisions. You have shown superior wisdom in your choice of friends. You do know how to associate with quality people. I like that. I want you to know that I love you more than anything or anyone in the whole wide world as my daughter. I hope you never suffer pain, for I would hurt more than you. I hope that you never get too disappointed for I would sink deeper in grief than you would. You must be happy for that's the only way I can be truly happy. You are a good girl. You are pretty and you deserve the best always. You work hard and should receive ample dividends. As you approach your 18th birthday, please know that your life as my daughter has always made me real proud. God has really blessed me by giving me you.

Love,

Mom

My mother gave me a gift that I will always treasure; her love for me expressed in written words. No matter what experiences or transitions that I experienced in my life, I always knew that this person loved me, unconditionally, and I had evidence to prove it. As you follow my parenting journey through the letters to my own daughter, I hope that you can identify similar experiences in your own parenting journey that you may want to document, convey or share.

Pearl of Wisdom

Unconditional love is real love

CHAPTER 1

Raising a Queen

As a small child, my daughter, Maria, was a very happy, tenacious and busy little person. She always lit up a room and enjoyed being in charge. My earliest memory of knowing that she wanted to be a great person was on career day at her pre-school. The teacher took individual photos of each child and wrote on the bottom of the picture the child's chosen career. The parents were asked to come to their class to view their career display. When I arrived to the classroom, I was fairly excited, because I was about to get a peek at my daughter's personal career aspirations. So, I walked to the display and eagerly searched for Maria's picture.

Most of the photos were labeled with doctor, lawyer, scientist, teacher, etc. Finally, I found my daughter's photo. There she was...adorned with a huge smile and feet dangling from the chair, hugging the largest stuffed animal available in the classroom with a huge smile on her face. My eyes went straight to the bottom of the picture. Maria's chosen career was "Queen". But I wasn't shocked at all that this was the chosen career of my 4-year old daughter. She may not have chosen a career path that seemed realistic to most people. But Maria had no doubt about how she wanted to feel.

Our children come into this world with a purpose and it's our responsibility to help identify their gifts and talents and guide them as they develop their natural gifts. To me, my daughter choosing "Queen" as her career of choice did not necessarily mean that she would become the Queen of England; but in this day in time, it could possibly happen. It meant to me that she had the pure, untarnished, confidence to be whatever she wanted to be in life and it was my job to support and protect her self-confidence and self-esteem.

Raising Queen Maria
To be the mother of Maria, the Queen,
Is a royal calling, you know what I mean?

To bring her in this world was a task of its own
But guiding her through life is a story untold

Her life's journey starts with proper
nurturing and care
Only to open her infancy
to a father not there

But her family's support doesn't miss a beat
Because the family's love runs so deep
Grandparents, aunts, uncles

and even cousins are there
Feeding, teaching and making memories to
share

Mom works hard, keeping a roof over their
heads
As God makes provisions
for what He's already said

A stepfather, soon, comes as an anchor in her
life
A kind, gentle man, who loves despite the price

This queen of a child has a calling on her life
Her energy is strong, and her spirit is right

Her beauty runs deep, inside and out
She's full of potential, without a doubt
Her interests carefully guided,
Without losing who she is
Keeping God in the midst of her laughter and
tears
Praying daily for her covering and

God's favor at all times

Keeps my heart at peace and tranquility in my mind

One could not wish for a better daughter to raise

But to live up to the calling

I give God all the praise

Ears have not heard, and eyes have not seen

God's great plans for my Maria, the Queen

As a mother, it is our role to observe, support and protect. As our daughters grow, we should learn their personalities and nurture their gifts. It is not our place to change who they are or live our lives through them. Be patient, be kind and be their mother. God will do the rest.

"For I know the plans that I have for you," declares the Lord, "plans to prosper you and not to harm you, plans to give you hope and a future.

Jeremiah 29:11

Pearl of Wisdom

Our daughters
become what they
believe; don't
shatter their
dreams

CHAPTER 2

Teen Talk

*P*arenting is rewarding but challenging at times. Mothers and daughters especially have challenges in the pre-teen and teenage years of their daughters' lives. Hormonal changes and the onset of puberty make verbal conversations a game of chance. If you put a group of mothers together who have teenage daughters, I'm sure that they could come up with a whole laundry list of similar communication and emotional challenges that they, too, have experienced. I'm sure there were challenging moments in my mother's parenting journey that made the list, as well. A mother's first experience of having a teenage daughter has a unique learning curve, like that of having your first child. The parent is learning as the child is growing. Even though a mother's parenting style has a lot to do with their background, culture and how they were raised, a parent has the freedom to design their own parenting rubric.

When I found myself in the middle of a conversation with my pre-teen daughter that seemed to be going nowhere and built around a total misunderstanding between both parties, I knew that it was time to step back and start writing.

First, I would process what I thought my daughter was trying to tell me and then attempted to write my thoughts in response to what I thought she was feeling. I learned over the years that understanding how a person feels is the foundation of good communication.

So, on February 18, 2004, I wrote this letter to my 14-year-old daughter. I didn't know if she would read it at that moment; but she always gave me the respect of her full attention by eventually reading my written words when her heart was ready.

Dear Maria,

As you know, I express myself better in writing. I apologize for upsetting you. You are probably right about me being a sensitive person. And you are probably even more right about me being even more sensitive when it comes to subjects dealing with you. But you are my first born and only daughter and I love you more than you will ever know.

As a mother, I do have personal dreams for your life. After all, I did bring you into this world. But I also understand that you are growing up now and you will have your own dreams and desires.

Maybe I do try too hard sometimes. If you want me to, I'll back off and give you more space. You have been able to make your own decisions and learn from your mistakes. I don't think that at this time in your life you will understand my perspective on everything and you may not understand the depth of a mother's love; but one day, you will be able to look back and understand a glimmer of what I was trying to teach you.

I don't have all the answers. But I feel that I have done the best I know how to do. So, I am at peace. I don't want you to be in danger or put yourself in the position to potentially be hurt by others; but I must trust God to protect you and release you to His care.

You are a strong young woman and great daughter. I value you and everything you put your heart into. You are a great leader in the church, school and community. I'm proud of you. Take Care of Yourself.

Love You,

Mom

When mother-daughter apologies are made, and the process of forgiveness begins, misunderstandings, negativity and resentment have no power. Hormones balance out and love prevails. Motherhood and daughterhood are worlds of second chances. We learn and grow together.

Pearl of Wisdom

Sincere apologies
are the foundation
of true forgiveness
and strong
relationships

CHAPTER 3

Managing Communication Breakdown

*A*s a mother moves through her daughter's pre-teen ages, she then proceeds to the era of parenting a full-blown teenager. Parenting anxiety can increase as communication breakdown increases. So, the beginning of active listening and compromise starts. On December 16, 2004, I wrote this letter to my sixteen-year-old daughter:

Dear Maria,

First, I would like to say that I am glad that you finally came and expressed your feelings to me last night. I wasn't aware you were feeling that way. Whatever I did or whatever you thought I did was not intentional. I apologize.

What I do want to say to you is that I love you very much and would not do or say anything that I think would harm you in any kind of way. Sometimes I'm right and sometimes I'm wrong. I do not claim to be a perfect mother. I just continue daily to the calling of guiding and protecting you the best way I know how.

Sometimes, my only consolation is in knowing that God is and will continue to be the perfect guide and protector for you now and the rest of your life.

You've always said that you appreciate what your parents have done to provide for you by giving you the things that you need and many things that you want. Even though I'm thankful for God enabling us to provide for our children, sometimes when life is made so easy, we dwell on the things that are not as important to be unhappy.

Maria, whether you feel like it or not at this moment, you are blessed. You may not feel like your life is perfect; but life is not supposed to be perfect. God allows some obstacles in our life to show us that He is still in control. We learn as we grow older how to handle these challenges that are placed before us.

I've learned as I've grown older, that my joy and peace must come from within me. If I waited for someone else to value my talents, my work, my accomplishments or who I am as a person, I would constantly be disappointed throughout my life. What's great about being a child of God is that He loves us unconditionally, no matter what. So, when the people you love or like or respect or admire, disappoint you, always remember that only God's opinion really matters.

Mothers may not always have the most profound words; but they should always come from a loving and true place in their hearts. Knowing what to say in an emotional situation may not always be easy. The first step is to listen to your daughter, try to understand their perspective and then self-evaluate before you offer your advice. Sometimes an immediate verbal response will work; but when emotions are sensitive, your sincere apology first and then your written advice is most effective.

Pearl of Wisdom

Every conversation
has its own identity.
Be careful to listen
first and then
respond.

CHAPTER 4

Decision Making

How do mothers talk to their daughters about decision-making, when they don't feel like they've always made the best decisions in their lives? Well, you start with what you know and advise from your own experiences. If none of these things apply, then there's always a scripture of reference that will work for any situation. On May 18, 2005, I felt like it was time to be proactive and share with my daughter a plan for decision-making as she moved into her Senior year of high school.

...whatever things are true, whatever things are noble, whatever things are just, whatever things are pure, whatever things are lovely, whatever

things are of good report, if there be any virtue and if there is anything praiseworthy, think on these things. Philippians 4:8

Dear Maria,

You are in charge of your life. You are ultimately responsible for your decisions. Good decisions and poor decisions separate the successful from the unsuccessful. We, as parents, can't make all decisions for you. But my prayer is that you will listen to the voice of the Holy Spirit to guide your choices throughout your life. Your life is in your hands; and the consequences of your decisions are also in your hands.

My role, as a mother, is to guide you in the right direction and educate you about things that may seem innocent to experiment with, but potentially harmful to you. The ultimate decision will be made by you. You must choose which road to travel. Whether rocky or straight, it will be your road. Continue to stay focused on your goals and don't let distractions of the world detain you from getting what you want out of life. I love you and want the best for you. It gives me great joy when I know that you are making good choices. I hope that you will continue to respect me and respect yourself. Love You.

Your Mom,

Pearl of Wisdom

Own your decisions;
they are your
responsibility

CHAPTER 5

Who Holds My Tomorrow?

My daughter's teenage years were filled with life and many school activities. She was just as busy and active as she was as a younger child. She had a contagious laugh that won the hearts of many and she worked hard to help her friends, classmates and community. Even though, I knew that Maria and her friends were smart girls, the mother in me, always worried that their kindness could be interpreted as weakness and good decision-making could be compromised. So, in one of my deep thought moments, I wrote this poem, not just for Maria, but also for her closest friends.

As I glance at where I've been,

The paths that were taken,

The decisions that were made,

And the future they were making,

Always trying to cling to what was right,

Never choosing a way

Without an escape route in sight

My thoughts, my fears, covering my voice,

With the echoes of my ancestors

shadowing my choice

The weight of the world

seems to lay heavy on my back

The enemy continuing to stay on my track

Do I allow the world to control what I do?

Or do I stand fast and firm

To what I know to be true?

Do I vow to take control of every step that I
take?

Every word that I say,

And every choice that I make?

Do I allow my tomorrow

To be scarred by my past?

Instead of embracing what's ahead

And what I know will truly last

Every day is a new chance to live, love and grow

My decisions mixed with God's wisdom

Is the weapon that I show

I can't afford to make loose decisions

At the risk of failing the test

My life, free of lukewarm living

Is God at His best

Who holds my tomorrow?

My decisions everyday

A life in line with God's purpose

Is the prayer that I pray

A reflection of God's Word

Is what my life should say

Granting me a beautiful tomorrow

And a forgiven yesterday

Pearl of Wisdom

You are in control of
your tomorrow;
Everyday is a new
day

CHAPTER 6

Money Matters

*T*his letter that was written to my daughter was a little out of my area of expertise; but It was time to address the topic of money. My daughter was turning 18 years old soon and surprisingly, credit card offers had already started to roll in. I had never considered myself a money expert and frankly, still learning; but I wanted her to understand the risks of credit card usage and picked up a few facts that I thought would give her a head-start on avoiding common mistakes that I had made and those things that would give her a financial edge over the average person her age. On August 3, 2005, I attempted to give her a crash course in financial management; specifically, credit card chaos.

Hi Maria,

You're turning 18 soon. You will be receiving credit card offers from different retail establishments and credit card companies soon. For you to avoid going into credit card usage blindly, I would like to give you a brief overview of credit cards to help you make wise decisions, at an early age; so that your dreams and goals won't be hindered by careless debt.

Fact I-Credit card offers target young adults and especially college students

Fact II- Most credit cards charge an annual fee, even if you don't use them

Fact III-Credit card companies can charge you 21%-25% interest on credit card balances. If paying minimum payments on balances, it could take 20 years to pay off a credit card.

Fact IV-Credit card companies allow you to charge past your credit limits and charge you for going over your limit.

Fact V-Using credit cards as an extension of your income can become very dangerous to a person's financial stability.

I'm not an expert in financial management; but I hope that these words of wisdom will guide you in the right direction as you continue on your road of financial success and happiness in the future.

Love You,

Mom

Pearl of Wisdom

Don't spend, what
you don't have;
live within your means

CHAPTER 7

Graduation Guidance

The summer of 2006 was a transitional time in my parenting journey. My daughter had just graduated from high school and this was the last summer before she was to leave for college. It was also the busiest summer of my daughter's teenage years. She was active in about ten different organizations; including church, social and academic organizations. She was being pulled in many directions and her acceptance to Spelman College seemed to attract friends and foes who had not been there before, in the past. My mother was still living at the time and she saw that I was getting uneasy about the time with my daughter leaving right before my eyes. We had shared our mother-daughter time with the church and community and even other families that loved to have Maria around; and our time together was narrowing more and more daily and we weren't taking much time to sit down and talk. My mother assured me that even though it seemed like others were taking the precious moments I had left during my daughter's last summer at home before leaving for college, she would be my daughter forever. At that moment, I was at peace and decided to share my heart to heart conversation to my daughter before leaving for college on paper. I wrote my thoughts to my daughter on June 21, 2006.

Dear Maria,

When I think of what I'd want to tell you before you leave for college, my mind just becomes cluttered. There are so many things that come to my mind; with no one thing being more important than the other. First, I want you to know that I am so proud of you. I could not have ordered a more gifted, talented and spiritually mature daughter than you, if I tried. You have truly been my teacher and my daily inspiration. It has been an honor to be your mother, mentor and your friend.

When you were an "arm baby" a woman came up to me and said that you would do great things in life and be a great leader. She also told me that if I kept the Word of God in front of you that nothing or anyone would harm you. As soon as she told me those words, she disappeared. To this day, I don't know who that woman was; but I know that her message tome was sent by God.

Throughout your childhood, you have always shown maturity and wisdom beyond your years. Your "sassy" ways were embraced by some and rejected by others; but the people that really understood you, loved everything about you.

I gave you to the Lord a long time ago, and he has guided me in every decision that I have had to make in raising you. He has not failed me yet, and I am confident that He will continue to cover and protect you and give you favor in the years to come.

When I think of advice to give you before you leave home, I immediately reflect on those things that I wish I had of known before I left home; like money management, being more frugal, goal setting, good study skills and healthy living. But we both know that until a person is ready to receive helpful information and make it a priority of change, it's a waste of time and energy.

So, instead of getting on my "soap box", I would like to talk about things that are really important. Relationships. Life is about relationships. Your relationship with God, family, friends, teachers, mentors, classmates, roommates, boyfriends, husbands, neighbors, etc...

The golden rule still applies, "Do unto others as you would have them do unto you..." Matthew 7:12. This means that you should always treat other people as you would want them to treat you in the same situation.

"Be anxious for nothing..." Philippians 4:6-7.

This is one of the hardest rules to live by. It is so tempting to try to work things out for God, prematurely. It is human nature to try to fix things or give up before God's says so.

"We wrestle not against flesh and blood, but against principalities..." Ephesians 6:12. This means that when someone comes up against us in any way, we must look beyond that person and realize that it is just the "devil" using them to try to break us down at our weakest moment (especially that time of the month!).

"We are more than conquerors through Christ!" Romans 8:37. This means that no matter what the situation, no matter what the test, in the end, we will come out victorious.

Maria, I love you. I hope that you can reflect on what you have been taught and build a wonderful life for yourself. My vision for you goes far beyond what you or I can see. But I know that "You can do all things through Christ who strengthens you..." Philippians 4:13

Love You,

Mom

As a mother, letting go of your daughter and allowing her to step out and put in practice what you've shown her and taught her can make a mother feel uneasy. You naturally worry about their safety and protection and how they will handle those things and situations that come their way. That's when you must trust what you've already invested in your daughter and know that your prayers will sustain her now and forever.

Pearl of Wisdom

God's Word will
sustain you when
no one else or
nothing else will

CHAPTER 8

Leaving the Nest

To some, an empty nest means that the children are leaving the home, going to college, starting their professions and the parents can start doing those personal things that may have once been put on hold as they were raising their children; but to a mother, that next stage of parenting can be bitter-sweet.

You're excited that your child is growing up and everything that you have instilled in them will now be tested in real-life situations; but that's when the motherhood anxiety kicks in! The next letter expresses those mixed feelings and mini-life lesson reviews that I wanted to share again on their way out of the nest.

Dear Maria,

This is one of the hardest stages of parenting for a mother; when a child leaves the nest. You haven't completely left the nest yet; but I feel like I'm emotionally already there.

Our relationship is important to me and the thought of having to share you with the world makes me a little sad; but this is a painful, yet necessary transition.

This letter is to let you know that it is ok for you to take your wings. I know that you will be introduced to a whole new world out there. Some things will fall in line with what I believe and what I choose to do; but some will not. As a mother, I will work hard to release you to make your own personal choices and be there when you need me. If you need me for anything, just know that I'm always here.

Love Always,

Your Mom

Pearl of Wisdom

To love you is to raise you and release you to fulfill God's purpose for your life

CHAPTER 9

Flying On Her Own

*N*ow, your child has left the nest and now flying on their own. As a mother, it feels like when the training wheels are taken off a bicycle and your child is peddling on their own. The parent is cheering them on and while watching, just in case the fall and need their assistance to get back on the bicycle. It's exciting and scary at the same time.

This letter was written the summer after my daughter's first year in college. Get out of the way Mom, it's time for her to fly!

Dear Maria,

This summer is going so well! You had an excellent freshman year at Spelman College. You have a great summer internship at Fed Ex! Ron, Jr. had a great year in middle school at Snowden and he loves his architecture camp at U of M. Overall, things seem to be lining up in our favor, in every aspect of our lives. I thank God for covering our family, guiding us and working out things that may seem impossible.

You are now at a point in your life where every decision that you make will affect your success and how fast or slow you reach your life goals. Your destiny is in your hands. This can be exciting, but it can also be intimidating and overwhelming. This newfound freedom of decision-making is a big-ticket item. It's very valuable; but if purchased too early or used loosely, can take a lifetime to pay off. Continue to use your freedom wisely.

I am excited about the happiness that you've found in your new relationship. When you are happy, I am happy. You are a smart young lady and I know that whoever you choose as a friend, boyfriend or mate will reflect the standards and values instilled in you and hopefully shown before you. If a person truly loves you, you will not have to chase after their affection. You will be a priority to them. The relationship will not breed stress or anxiety. It will naturally flow with a balance of love, peace and joy.

As you step into the beginning of adulthood, be careful to protect your character, integrity and testimony. The enemy and the spirit of fear are aware of your success, your potential and your commitment to God and seeks and waits for the right opportunity to bring you down, defer your dreams and divert the plans that God has laid out for you. But God, so kindly, provides a way of escape and gives us the Holy Spirit to guide us through our toughest decisions.

Ephesians 6:11-18 says, "Keep on the whole armor of God, so that you are able to stand... gird your waist with the truth, the breastplate of righteousness, your feet with the preparation of *peace, shield of faith and the helmet of salvation and the sword of the Spirit, which is the Word of God...and pray...*

With Love,

Your Mom

Pearl of Wisdom

Stay focused...
Do Right, Move Forward
and Soar

CHAPTER 10

Letting Her Soar

As a young mother and professional, I always understood science, to be exact. Therefore, just like formulas and equations explain theories and phenomena, I thought that my professional life, family life, and parenting could be just as predictable with the correct formula. My theory was absolutely wrong! There is no perfect formula for parenting. If there were, knowing the formula and implementing a formula are two different things.

I learned that parenting is a divine assignment that is given to you without a step-by-step rule book. God allows you to be the caretaker of His child and Mother Earth is their playground.

As you oversee the life of your daughter, this journey is preparation for the day you've enough as a parent to let go and allow them to move forward into what God has purposed for their lives. It's not your plan; it's God's plan. This act alone can be the most challenging task and liberating task of parenthood.

The ability to release someone you love more than yourself to an unforgiving world is a leap of faith; but now, it's time for her to soar!

Dear Maria,

I am so proud of you! This letter comes at a time in your life when every decision you make is a springboard of where you will go next and sets the foundation for your future. You've sacrificed a lot and worked hard to stay on track. So, don't lose your place in line. You've shown so much strength this past year. Through the loss of family members, pledging AKA (Alpha Kappa Alpha, Inc.), and a busy summer filled with internships, you have prevailed. Some chapters in your life may feel lonely at times, but that's when the sermons, scriptures, and hymns of yesterday start making sense to you. Never Alone...I'm Happy with Jesus Alone...What a Friend We Have in Jesus... and the list goes on. Despite life's variables and challenges, everything has worked together for your good.

Thank you for being you. I couldn't have asked for a better daughter, Soror, and friend. I truly appreciate your commitment to excellence and hard work at school, work, and home. You are a jewel, and I love you very much. Continue to stay focused on your goals and put God first in all that you do. Maintain an attitude of gratitude and your life will give you more and more to be thankful for.

You are headed for greatness, and this coming school year is setting the foundation for your exponential launching pad. I am excited for you, and I am here for you when you need me. I love you, and there's nothing you can do or say to change that. When you're happy, I am happy. When you hurt, I hurt. That's the heart of a mother. So, never think you are alone. As long as I live, I am always praying on your behalf. You and generations after you will be blessed.

Love You Always,

Your Mom, Soror, and Friend

Conclusion

The gift of parenting is a mosaic of many colorful layers. Some parents begin their journey from the birth of their child, and some are blessed with their children through many other divine ways.

Whatever the vehicle of parental assignment may be, it is an awesome privilege and responsibility. Handle with caution and care. You are the chosen one to provide, guide, and protect this spiritual being.

Every day may not be perfect, and every parental decision may not seem immediately effective, but the Master Plan for your child's life is sketched in God's Universe, and it is good. So, embrace your calling as a parent with all confidence that you have been chosen for this extraordinary and sometimes challenging assignment. The journey is priceless.

Letter to My Daughter